EVERYDAY
RAW
EXPRESS

RECIPES IN 30 MINUTES OR LESS

MATTHEW KENNEY
PHOTOGRAPHS BY ADRIAN MUELLER

GIBBS SMITH
TO ENRICH AND INSPIRE HUMANKIND

First Edition
15 14 13 12 11   5 4 3 2 1

Text © 2011 Matthew Kenney
Photographs © 2011 Adrian Mueller

Published by
Gibbs Smith
P.O. Box 667
Layton, Utah 84041

1.800.835.4993 orders
www.gibbs-smith.com

Designed by Debra McQuiston
Printed and bound in Hong Kong

Gibbs Smith books are printed on paper produced from sustain-
able PEFC-certified forest/controlled wood source. Learn more
at www.pefc.org.

Library of Congress Cataloging-in-Publication Data:

Kenney, Matthew.
  Everyday raw express : recipes in 30 minutes or less /
Matthew Kenney ; photographs by Adrian Mueller. — 1st ed.
     p. cm.
  Includes index.
  ISBN 978-1-4236-1891-1 (alk. paper)
  1. Vegetarian cooking. 2. Raw foods. 3. Cookbooks. I. Title.
  TX837.K4644 2011
  641.5'636—dc22
                                        2011006767.

EVERYDAY
RAW
EXPRESS

contents

acknowledgments

Much like a family gathering or an annual reunion, our work with *Everyday Raw* has evolved into a dynamic and fun experience with a great deal of comfort. As I contemplate our recent production of *Everyday Raw Express*, which followed two predecessors, *Everyday Raw* and *Everyday Raw Desserts*, and anticipate the upcoming *Raw Chocolate*, I am most thankful for the collaborative effort and contributions of the core team we've built around this exciting series of books.

Perhaps as rewarding as holding the completed manuscript itself is the opportunity to work with such wonderfully talented people who create in a most harmonious way. The experience is one in which the outcome always feels as natural as the raw, organic food within its pages. We now have a production rhythm that convenes in Maine; involves countless long days of food preparation, presentation, and photography; and ends late at night with great wines and a roaring fire.

Anyone who is familiar with my recent projects will recognize Meredith Baird as a driving force within my company, and with each passing month, her influence is greater. She has developed a contemporary style that combines great skill and taste not only with food, but with aesthetics and even organization—a much-needed skill for successful book production. Whereas Meredith played a very large role in *Everyday Raw Desserts*, she was the driving force behind *Everyday Raw Express*. Because of her tireless and brilliant efforts and dedication, this book is a shining example of how wonderful simple raw food can be.

Our books are forever lifted by incredible photography within their pages and Adrian Mueller has taken this gift to the next level, with his incredible attention to detail, unshakeable professionalism, and ability to capture light like no one I've worked with. He has been a tremendous collaborator, friend, and quite respectable golfing partner.

Jessica Acs joins us from Canada this year by plane, train, and automobile. She not only possesses great taste and culinary skills, but also serves as a wonderful, warm, and centered balance to our production. She is a thoughtful and great friend, and her yoga and stretching lessons could not come at a better time.

Brian Roberts worked with Meredith and me the entire summer—testing, sourcing, and holding our chaotic kitchen together. We thank him for joining our group and welcome him back for *Raw Chocolate*.

I'm incredibly grateful to my editor, Jennifer Adams, who has my full confidence not only to bring the many elements of our books together, but to enhance them in a way that I'm always waiting in eager anticipation for the galleys to arrive, knowing full well that she will have sculpted a beautiful work from the many diverse elements she has to work with.

As we begin work on our fifth book together, I am thrilled to be working with the team at Gibbs Smith, Publisher: Gibbs Smith, Jennifer King Durrant, Christopher Robbins, and the entire team who produce one incredible book after another. I look forward to the next five books!

Without my many supportive business partners, team members, students, and a great system, I would not have time to be involved in these exciting books. Thank you all for managing our companies with such passion.

Finally, to my family: Shirley, Robert, and Patrick Kenney; and Maryellen and Paul Shchoeman. Thanks for understanding that a hunter from Maine could end up as a vegetarian chef.

—Matthew

I would like to express my appreciation to my lovely mom and sister; to Jessica, one of my dearest friends; and, of course, to Matthew, my partner and friend who continues to support me in so many ways—and without whom none of this would be possible.

—Meredith

introduction

While raw food is largely known for its growing presence in upscale restaurants and through its beautiful and colorful imagery in cookbooks, many recipes by raw food chefs are admittedly complicated or time-consuming to make. Even many of the simpler variations still require long periods of dehydrating and, occasionally, ingredients that are difficult to find and work with. There is no denying that the effort to prepare these dishes can be well worth it, but there are times and places that simply don't allow for the process, ingredients, or equipment. As someone with a busy professional schedule, I can easily empathize with anyone wishing to experience gourmet raw food at home, but in a faster, simpler manner. *Everyday Raw Express* is written with this goal in mind.

This may be the most challenging book we've written and, in many ways, the most rewarding: regardless of the complexity or simplicity of a recipe, we are always deeply committed to creating dishes that are full flavored, original, and vibrant. Our goal was to write a book that allowed for these standards to be met, while offering recipes that are largely prepared in less than half an hour, with no dehydrating whatsoever. Though we love young coconuts, we also decided to write a book without them, given that many of you do not have readily available sources for them, and the fact that there is a lot of labor involved in opening and using them. We've also tried our best to reduce the percentage of recipes with nuts—although we love them too, simple recipes benefit from a bit of lightening. Overall, the dishes themselves are just as dynamic, if not more so, than their complicated counterparts.

We consider this a step toward the advancement of raw cuisine, in that it allows us to develop it in a way that it is more accessible and practical. It would be impossible for us to create these dishes without first having been very experimental and learning so much about the possibilities of this fascinating plant-based lifestyle. It is our goal that the recipes and techniques you'll find in our new book will help you incorporate more gourmet raw food into your home kitchen, as well as provide ideas for you to experiment with and create on your own.

Our Express Philosophy

As is always the case with our cuisine, ingredients remain the most valuable asset involved in its creation. This is even more true when preparing recipes with clean, refined techniques like those used in this book. While we can offer creative options to prepare raw food simply, the results will still largely depend on the quality of your ingredients. A perfectly ripe heirloom tomato with just a touch of olive oil and sea salt can taste like one of the most incredible works of art, while an out-of-season and under-ripe tomato may be completely off-putting, despite the exact same presentation and techniques being used.

Great food starts with great ingredients—always. Therefore, we strongly encourage you to learn everything you can about seasonality, utilizing ingredients when they are at their peak, and exploring your immediate area to find the best local ingredients, farmers markets, and artisanal products, all of which will greatly enhance the results of your culinary efforts.

If there is one operating philosophy to follow when preparing these recipes, it is the goal of passionately pursuing the best that local, seasonal, and organic have to offer. Make this sourcing your mission and you'll never regret it.

How to Use This Book

A good recipe should be seen as a road map, offering guidance and technique toward combining foods. But, ultimately, you should use your own preferences freely to make adjustments. These may include ingredient substitutions, seasoning or plating variations, or even an entirely new dish using the technique of another.

Some chefs may not wish for their recipes to be tampered with, but we encourage it. Depending on where you are in the world, you may have products that can actually enhance our original recipe, or you may have an idea that we haven't thought of. I always love it when I hear someone explaining how they have adjusted my recipe, and, more than once, I've been very impressed with the results.

Familiarize yourself with the methods used in these pages, and you'll find yourself with endless ideas for additional recipes. Be fearless, enjoy the process, and always follow your instincts.

IRS

Lemongrass Pear Tonic

Various combinations of vegetable, fruit, and aromatics work well in this style of elixir.

2 pears
2 stalks celery
1 stalk lemongrass

Run all ingredients through a juicer. Serve chilled.

SERVES 2

Spy-C Lemonade

This is a slight variation on the classic Master Cleanse. It's great for cleansing or to sip on during a day of fasting.

½ cup lemon juice
1 apple, juiced
¼ cup honey, agave, or maple syrup
1 teaspoon cayenne
1 quart water (sparkling or still)

Mix all ingredients. Serve chilled, over ice.

SERVES 2–4

Green Juice

The staple beverage for many living a healthy lifestyle, green juice does benefit from a bit of fruit, which makes it far more appealing and pleasant to drink.

8 to 10 large dark green leaves
   (kale, collards, Swiss chard, or a
   combination)
½ bunch cilantro
2 stalks celery
1 apple
½ lemon, peeled
1-inch piece ginger

Run all ingredients through a juicer. Serve slightly chilled.

SERVES 2–4

Cucumber Refresher

A small shot is ideal before a meal or when you wake up in the morning.

2 medium cucumbers
2 limes, peeled
1/4 medium pineapple, peeled

Run all ingredients through a juicer. Serve slightly chilled.

SERVES 2–4

Ginger Ale

Not to be confused with Schweppes, but refreshing and spritzy nonetheless.

¼ cup ginger juice
1 apple, juiced
¼ cup lemon juice
¼ cup honey, agave, or maple syrup
1 quart sparkling water

Mix all juices and sweetener. Fill glasses half full with juice mixture. Top with sparkling water.

SERVES 2–4

Apple Cider

For a cooler climate, we recommend serving this slightly warmed.

2 cups apple juice (approximately
    6 medium apples)
¼ cup honey, agave, or maple syrup
¼ cup apple cider vinegar
1 teaspoon cinnamon
½ teaspoon nutmeg
Pinch cayenne

Blend all ingredients.

SERVES 2–4

Ginger Ale

Grapefruit Mojito

Not only is this good on its own, but also with a touch of dry sake, as a cocktail.

2 cups grapefruit juice
1 handful mint leaves
¼ cup agave nectar
1 cup ice cubes
1 cup sparkling water
Thinly sliced grapefruit rounds

Muddle grapefruit juice, mint, and agave. Divide between two glasses. Top with ice and sparkling water. Garnish with grapefruit rounds.

SERVES 2

Fire Starter

Ginger and cayenne are not only warming, but also great for digestion and cleansing. Adjust the quantities according to your taste and tolerance for heat.

2 cups orange juice (approximately
   8 oranges)
2 tablespoons lemon juice
1-inch piece ginger, juiced
Pinch cayenne
2 to 3 drops oregano oil

Mix all ingredients. Best served chilled.

SERVES 2

Grapefruit Mojito

Red Beet Sangria

Of course, we all know sangria from its wine-friendly roots, and this recipe is no exception. It's excellent with red wine.

2 cups beet juice (approximately
  3 to 4 medium beets)
1 cup orange juice
1 cup apple or pear juice
1 cinnamon stick
Pinch cayenne
¼ cup agave (optional)
2 cups chopped fruit (apples,
  oranges, limes, or melon)

Mix juices, spices, and agave, if using, in a large pitcher. Add chopped fruit and stir. Allow to marinate, chilled, for at least 30 minutes.

SERVES 2–4

Electrolyte Margarita

This elixir is also delicious with a dry sake, and even with a touch of sparkling wine.

3 to 4 limes, peeled
2 tablespoons coconut butter
¼ cup honey, agave, or maple syrup
3 to 4 cups cold water or chilled
  coconut water
Pinch salt

Blend all ingredients until smooth and frothy. Serve immediately.

SERVES 2–4

Red Beet Sangria

EXPRESS
SMOO

THIES

Blueberry, Lavender

As with all of our recipes, we encourage making adjustments seasonally and according to the quality of available ingredients. Any berry—even other greens—works equally well in this fragrant smoothie.

5 cups blueberries, fresh or frozen
2 cups almond milk
1 handful spinach (approximately
   1 cup)
1 tablespoon honey
1 tablespoon dried lavender
1 teaspoon vanilla
Pinch salt

Blend all ingredients in a high-speed blender until smooth.

SERVES 2–4

Mango, Goji, Basil

A cleansing recipe, this would also be great with a pinch of cayenne pepper.

4 cups chopped mango
½ cup goji berries
1 to 2 cups water or coconut water
2-inch piece aloe, peeled
¼ cup basil leaves
1 tablespoon honey, agave, or
   maple syrup

Blend all ingredients in a high-speed blender until smooth.

SERVES 2–4

Raspberry, Hibiscus

Conceptually, chilled brewed tea is a great base for a light smoothie, adding an element of savory complexity.

4 cups raspberries, fresh or frozen
1 banana, frozen
1 cup hibiscus tea, freshly brewed
    and chilled
¼ cup mint
1 tablespoon honey, agave, or
    maple syrup
1 teaspoon vanilla
Pinch salt

Blend all ingredients in a high-speed blender until smooth.

SERVES 2–4

Grapefruit, Mint

Ripe, sweet pink or ruby red varieties of grapefruit are preferable for this recipe.

2 grapefruits, peeled
2 bananas, frozen
1-inch piece ginger
1 cup mint
1 to 2 cups water or coconut water
1 tablespoon honey, agave, or
    maple syrup
1 teaspoon vanilla
Pinch salt

Blend all ingredients in a high-speed blender until smooth.

SERVES 2–4

Pineapple, Ginger, Spice

When bananas are very ripe, peel, chop, and store them in the freezer (covered or in sandwich bags). They make an ideal replacement for ice cubes, which can dilute flavor in smoothies and fruity drinks.

3 cups chopped pineapple, fresh or
   frozen
2 bananas, frozen
1-inch piece ginger
¼ cup mint leaves
1 to 2 cups water or coconut water
1 to 2 teaspoons diced red chile
1 tablespoon honey, agave, or
   maple syrup
Pinch salt

Blend all ingredients in a high-speed blender until smooth.

SERVES 2–4

Asian Pear, Green Tea

If Asian pears are unavailable, another green pear (or even apples) would work well as a replacement.

5 Asian pears, chopped (approximately 5 cups)
1 medium cucumber, peeled
1 lime, peeled
1 to 2 cups green tea, freshly brewed
1 tablespoon honey, agave, or maple syrup
1 teaspoon vanilla
Pinch salt

Blend all ingredients in a high-speed blender until smooth.

SERVES 2–4

Apple, Almond, Spice

There are numerous variations that work well with this recipe. Try peach and coriander in summer for example.

5 apples, cut in quarters and cored
2 cups almond milk
1 tablespoon chopped fresh
  rosemary
1 teaspoon cinnamon
1 tablespoon honey, agave, or
  maple syrup
1 teaspoon vanilla
Pinch salt

Blend all ingredients in a high-speed blender until smooth.

SERVES 2–4

Banana, Cacao

If we recommend any of our smoothies as a meal replacement, this is the one.

3 bananas, frozen (approximately
  5 cups)
¼ cup cacao powder
¼ cup cacao nibs
2 cups almond milk
¼ cup mint
1 to 2 tablespoons maca
1 tablespoon honey, agave, or
  maple syrup
1 teaspoon vanilla
Pinch salt

Blend all ingredients in a high-speed blender until smooth.

SERVES 2–4

Black Cherry, Hemp

Think of it as a chocolate-covered cherry.

4 cups pitted black cherries, fresh
   or frozen
2 cups hemp milk
¼ cup cacao nibs
1 tablespoon honey, agave, or
   maple syrup
Pinch salt

Blend all ingredients in a high-speed blender
until smooth.

SERVES 2–4

Watermelon, Arugula

This is more of a slushy in terms of flavor—
something that can be enhanced even further if you
happen to have a few cubes of frozen coconut water
on hand.

6 to 7 cups chopped watermelon,
   seeded
1 to 2 cups arugula
2 tablespoons lime juice
1 tablespoon honey, agave, or
   maple syrup
1 teaspoon vanilla
Pinch salt

Blend all ingredients in a high-speed blender
until smooth.

SERVES 2–4

Black Cherry, Hemp

EXPRESS

SOU

Summer Squash, Coriander Sour Cream

Feel free to prepare this with zucchini or a combination of zucchini and squash.

4 cups peeled and chopped yellow squash*
1/4 cup pine nuts
1 tablespoon nutritional yeast
3 tablespoons lemon juice
1 tablespoon agave
2 1/2 cups water (approximately)
1/2 teaspoon coriander
1 teaspoon salt
1 tablespoon olive oil
1/2 cup sour cream (page 122)

Blend all ingredients except olive oil and sour cream in a high-speed blender until smooth. Add olive oil at the last minute to emulsify. Garnish with sour cream.

*One large squash equals approximately 2 cups when peeled and chopped.

SERVES 2–4

Avocado Velouté

To lighten or add texture to the velouté, try adding your favorite chopped vegetables, such as tomatoes, fresh chiles, or peppers.

3 avocados
2 cups nut milk
1 cup water
1/2 cup cilantro leaves
1/2 tablespoon white miso
2 tablespoons lemon juice
Salt and pepper
Cilantro Oil (page 124) (optional)

Blend all ingredients in a high-speed blender until smooth. Season with salt and pepper to taste. Garnish with Cilantro Oil if desired.

SERVES 2–4

Watercress and Baby Spinach Soup

If the popular Green Goddess dressing were a soup, this would be it.

2 avocados, halved
1 cup watercress
1 cup baby spinach
2 tablespoons chopped parsley
1 tablespoon olive oil
1 teaspoon white miso
2 tablespoons lemon juice
1/4 teaspoon cayenne
3 to 4 cups water or nut milk
Salt and pepper

Blend all ingredients except half of one avocado in a high-speed blender until smooth. Season with salt and pepper to taste. Dice reserved avocado half to garnish soup.

SERVES 2–4

Moroccan Carrot, Golden Raisin Relish

For a lighter soup, the almond milk may be replaced with water or coconut water.

3 cups carrot juice
1 cup almond milk
1 avocado
1/4 cup lemon juice
1 tablespoon honey
1 tablespoon minced ginger
1/8 teaspoon allspice
2 tablespoons green olives (such as Picholine), slivered
1/4 cup Golden Raisin Relish (page 120)

Blend all ingredients other than olives and relish in a high-speed blender until smooth. Garnish with olives and relish.

SERVES 2–4

Gazpacho, Basil Sorbet

Adding a frozen component to spicy or tangy recipes such as gazpacho will have a mellowing and balancing effect. The textures in this dish are both complementary and also complex.

GAZPACHO

3 cups seeded and pureed heirloom tomatoes
1 cup seeded and chopped heirloom tomatoes
1 cup chopped tomatillos
2 tablespoons lime juice
½ red bell pepper, chopped
½ jalapeño pepper, diced
1 tablespoon olive oil
½ cup cilantro leaves
Salt and pepper

BASIL SORBET

½ cup agave
½ cup water
15 basil leaves, coarsely chopped (approximately)
½ cup lime juice
¼ cup coconut oil, melted

GAZPACHO Toss tomato puree with chopped tomatoes and remaining ingredients. Season with salt and pepper to taste.

BASIL SORBET Blend all ingredients in a high-speed blender until smooth. Pour into an ice cream maker and follow manufacturer's instructions.

ASSEMBLY For an extra hot day, serve soup with a scoop of basil sorbet in the center.

SERVES 2–4

Cream Corn Chowder, Jalapeño Parsley Pesto

While fresh sweet corn is preferable, we do recommend using frozen rather than canned. A small dice of avocado is also nice to top this chowder.

CHOWDER
4 cups yellow corn (fresh or frozen)
¼ cup pine nuts
2 cups nut milk
1 tablespoon miso
3 tablespoons olive oil
2 tablespoons lemon juice
¼ cup agave
Jalapeño Parsley Pesto (page 120)
Salt and pepper

Blend all ingredients except Jalapeño Parsley Pesto in a high-speed blender until smooth. Season with salt and pepper to taste. Serve with a dollop of Pesto.

SERVES 4

Creamy Mushroom Soup

For a richer soup, feel free to substitute a portion of water with nut milk.

2 cups assorted meaty mushrooms
  (baby bellas and trumpets work well)
1½ cups cashews
½ cup pine nuts
¼ cup white miso
1 tablespoon fresh tarragon
1 tablespoon olive oil
6 cups water
Salt and pepper
2 tablespoons roughly chopped
  parsley

Blend all ingredients other than parsley in a high-speed blender until smooth. Season with salt and pepper to taste. Garnish with chopped parsley.

SERVES 4

Cream Corn Chowder,
Jalapeño Parsley Pesto

Cream of Miso, Shiitake, Sea Vegetables

We typically think of miso soup as very light and often a good beginning or end to a meal. However, miso's deep, nutty flavor lends itself well to heavier and richer preparations, especially creamy dressings and soups.

SOUP BASE
6 cups water
¼ cup white miso
1 cup pine nuts
¼ cup cashews
1 tablespoon agave
1 tablespoon dulse flakes
Salt and pepper

SHIITAKE
1 cup shiitakes
1 tablespoon olive oil
1 tablespoon nama shoyu
1 tablespoon lemon juice

GARNISH
¼ cup hijiki, rehydrated and drained
¼ cup wakame, rehydrated and drained (finely chopped if you prefer smaller pieces)
Gomashio for garnish (optional)

SOUP Blend all ingredients in a high-speed blender until smooth. Season with salt and pepper to taste.

SHIITAKE Mix shiitakes with olive oil, nama shoyu, and lemon juice. Allow to marinate for at least 30 minutes.

FINISH Before serving, stir shiitake, hijiki, and wakame into blended cream. Garnish with gomashio if desired.

SERVES 4–6

Warm Kelp Soba, Sweet Dashi Broth

These kelp noodles are incredibly versatile and yet hard to find in stores. We recommend buying them directly from the company Sea Tangle (www.kelpnoodles.com).

BROTH

1½ cups water

1 cup nama shoyu

2 tablespoons dulse

1 tablespoon wakame

1 tablespoon sesame oil

1 tablespoon miso

2 tablespoons agave

1 tablespoon lemon juice

2 tablespoons chopped scallions

Gomashio (optional)

NOODLES

1 (32-ounce) bag of kelp noodles, rinsed and drained

BROTH Blend all ingredients in a high-speed blender until smooth and slightly warm. Strain through a fine sieve to remove any solids.

FINISH Equally portion out kelp noodles into bowls. Fill bowls with broth. Garnish with chopped scallions and gomashio if using.

SERVES 2–4

Curried Melon, Sour Cream, Pumpkin Seeds

If you have access to a market with high quality, fresh spices, we encourage you to experiment with making your own curry powders.

4 to 5 cups chopped and seeded
  cantaloupe or summer melon
1 avocado
2 tablespoons olive oil
1 tablespoon apple cider vinegar
¼ cup lemon juice
1 tablespoon nama shoyu
1 tablespoon minced ginger
1 tablespoon curry powder
½ teaspoon nutmeg
¼ teaspoon salt
Pinch cayenne
Salt and pepper
¼ cup sour cream (page 122)
1 cup pumpkin seeds, roughly
  chopped

Blend all ingredients other than sour cream and pumpkin seeds in a high-speed blender until smooth. Season with salt and pepper to taste. Garnish with a dollop of sour cream and sprinkle with pumpkin seeds.

SERVES 2–4

EXPRESS
STAR

TERS

Avocado Carpaccio

In most recipes, we recommend very ripe avocados. However, in this format, medium to just under-ripe will work best for presentation and texture.

DRESSING

¼ cup sesame oil
2 tablespoons sesame seeds (black or white)
2 tablespoons lemon juice
1 tablespoon nama shoyu
1 tablespoon agave
Salt and pepper

AVOCADO

2 to 3 avocados, halved, pitted, peeled, and thinly sliced lengthwise
1 handful micro basil (or other micro herb)
Sesame seeds (for garnish)
Coarse salt and pepper

Whisk all ingredients for dressing until well combined. Season with salt and pepper to taste.

Fan out approximately half an avocado per plate. Drizzle with dressing. Garnish with micro basil, sesame seeds, and coarse salt and pepper. Serve immediately.

SERVES 4

Candy Cane Beet Carpaccio, Citrus, Fennel Confit, Goat Cheese

Beets and citrus are almost always great paired together. In this recipe, any type of beets will make an acceptable substitution.

BEETS

1 pound candy cane beets
1 tablespoon olive oil
2 tablespoons red wine vinegar
1 tablespoon agave
Salt and pepper

FENNEL CONFIT

1 small fennel bulb
2 tablespoons olive oil
½ tablespoon agave
1 tablespoon lemon juice
2 teaspoons salt

GOAT CHEESE

1 cup cashews
1 cup macadamia nuts
1 tablespoon nutritional yeast
3 tablespoons lemon juice
1 teaspoon salt
1 teaspoon probiotic powder
  (optional)

BEETS Thinly slice beets on a mandoline (or by hand). It is essential that you have paper-thin slices. Toss with remaining ingredients and allow to marinate at least 30 minutes. If you can, marinate them 2 hours or up to overnight. The longer you allow them to marinate the better.

FENNEL CONFIT Quarter fennel lengthwise, then cut into long paper-thin strips (preferably on a mandoline). Toss with remaining ingredients and allow to marinate. Again, the longer the better.

GOAT CHEESE Blend all ingredients in a high-speed blender until smooth. If using the probiotic powder, line a bowl with cheesecloth and allow the cheese to drain at room temperature for 8 to 12 hours. Using the probiotic will make the cheese extra tart, but it is not a necessary step. If you aren't using the probiotic, you can serve the cheese immediately after blending.

FINISH Spread a thin layer of goat cheese on a plate. Lay a thin layer of beets on top of goat cheese spread. Garnish with fennel confit. Finish with a drizzle of extra marinade.

SERVES 4–6

Curried Carrot Slaw, Endive, Pine Nuts, Golden Raisins

Any lettuce cup would be a good substitute for endive, particularly radicchio when available.

DRESSING
½ cup cashews
2 tablespoons lime juice
2 tablespoons chopped ginger
1 tablespoon agave
1 tablespoon olive oil
1 tablespoon curry powder
1 teaspoon salt
1 cup water

SLAW
4 cups shredded carrots
½ cup golden raisins, chopped
¼ cup pine nuts
¼ cup mint

8 to 12 endive or radicchio leaves

DRESSING Blend all ingredients in a high-speed blender until smooth. Season with salt and pepper to taste. Reserve ¼ cup for garnish.

SLAW Toss dressing with shredded carrots, raisins, pine nuts, and mint. Chill at least 30 minutes. Ideally, allow to chill a few hours before serving.

FINISH Scoop slaw into endive or radicchio leaves and drizzle with reserved dressing. If desired, garnish with extra mint and a few pine nuts.

SERVES 4–6

Portobello, Serrano, Melon, Mint Syrup

Although this combination may seem a bit unusual, it derives from the classic dish of prosciutto and melon. The cool melon and mint balances the salty mushroom perfectly.

MUSHROOMS

4 portobello mushrooms, cleaned and thinly sliced in long strips
3 tablespoons olive oil
1 tablespoon lemon juice
1 serrano chile, seeded and minced
1 tablespoon nama shoyu
Salt and pepper

MINT SYRUP

1 cup mint, packed
2 tablespoons lemon juice
¼ cup agave

MELON

1 small melon thinly sliced in long strips comparable in size to the mushrooms

MUSHROOMS Toss portobello with oil, lemon, chile, and nama shoyu. Allow to marinate for at least 30 minutes to an hour. Season with salt and pepper before serving.

SYRUP Blend all ingredients in a high-speed blender until smooth.

FINISH Alternate portobello and thinly sliced melon. Drizzle with mint syrup and serve.

SERVES 4–6

Baby Zucchini and Avocado Tartar

This has become an instant favorite for multicourse dinners, where a simple, light, and beautifully presented dish is required.

2 firm avocados, finely diced
4 to 5 baby zucchini, finely diced
2 tablespoons lemon juice
1 tablespoon olive oil, plus more
   for garnish
2 tablespoons micro basil (or finely
   minced basil)
1 tablespoon minced chives, plus
   more for garnish
1 teaspoon agave
2 to 3 teaspoons coarse salt
Freshly ground pepper for garnish

Toss all ingredients until well combined. Divide into four servings and press into ring molds. Garnish with chives, fresh ground pepper, and a drizzle of olive oil.

SERVES 4

Heirloom Tomato, Seven-Herb Oil

Heirlooms, in peak season and especially when never refrigerated, need little more than a pinch of salt, great olive oil, and herbs for the best flavor. We always prefer to keep them simple.

DRESSING
1 tablespoon minced mint
1 teaspoon minced chives
1 teaspoon minced cilantro
1 teaspoon minced basil
1 teaspoon minced thyme
1 teaspoon minced oregano
1 teaspoon minced savory
1 cup olive oil

TOMATOES
2 to 3 large heirloom tomatoes, sliced (big enough to have 3 to 4 slices per serving)

GARNISH
Coarse salt
Pine nuts (optional)

Whisk oil and herbs together. Season with salt and pepper.

Lay out 3 to 4 tomato slices per serving. Drizzle generously with herb oil. Season generously with coarse salt and pine nuts if using.

SERVES 4

Wild Mushroom Pâté

Serve in endive or radicchio leaves. Or as an appetizer with crudités or your favorite crackers.

PÂTÉ

1 1/2 cups cleaned and chopped baby
    bella mushrooms
1/2 cup chopped walnuts
1 tablespoon olive oil
1 tablespoon lemon juice
1 tablespoon nama shoyu
1 tablespoon parsley
1 teaspoon thyme
1 teaspoon oregano
1 to 2 tablespoons water (more if
    needed)
1/2 teaspoon salt
1/8 teaspoon pepper

8 to 12 endive or radicchio leaves

Process all ingredients in a high-speed blender until mixed but chunky. Season with salt and pepper to taste. Scoop into endive or radicchio leaves to serve.

MAKES ABOUT 1 1/2 CUPS

EXPRESS

SALA

Frisée, Fennel, Walnuts, Cranberry, Maple Vinaigrette

Frisée, also known as chicory, became popular in French bistros when paired with smoky bacon, known as lardons. The use of fall flavors such as maple and cranberry in this recipe provide that autumnal accent that it is known for.

VINAIGRETTE

¼ cup balsamic, cider, or any good-quality vinegar
½ cup pure maple syrup
2 tablespoons lemon juice
2 tablespoons finely minced basil
1 cup olive oil
Salt and pepper

SALAD

6 to 8 cups frisée lettuce
1 small bulb fennel, thinly shaved on mandoline
1 cup walnuts, roughly chopped
½ cup dried cranberries, roughly chopped

VINAIGRETTE Whisk together vinegar, maple syrup, lemon juice, and basil. Add olive oil and continue to whisk until dressing is emulsified.

FINISH Delicately toss all ingredients with desired amount of dressing until well combined. Season with salt and pepper to taste. Garnish with extra walnuts, cranberries, and dressing if desired.

SERVES 4–6

Mâche, Pickled Cucumbers, Pistachios, Pistachio Oil

Chase's Daily in Maine serves a great summer salad with citrus and pistachio—we enjoyed it all summer, prompting this variation.

SALAD

6 to 8 cups mâche lettuce

1 cup pickled cucumbers, cut into quarters

½ cup pistachios, chopped

VINAIGRETTE

2 to 3 tablespoons lemon juice

¼ cup pistachio oil (or other nut oil)

Salt and pepper

Whisk together all ingredients for vinaigrette. Delicately toss all salad ingredients with vinaigrette. Generously season with coarse salt and pepper.

SERVES 4–6

Butter Lettuce, Flowers, Fines Herbes, Lemon Vinaigrette

This all-purpose salad is easy and fresh, and one that we make on a regular basis.

6 to 8 cups (or 6 to 8 big handfuls) butter or Bibb lettuce
1 to 2 handfuls fresh herbs (mint, basil, cilantro, savory), stems removed and lightly chopped
1 handful nasturtiums (optional)
2 to 3 tablespoons olive oil
3 to 4 tablespoons freshly squeezed lemon juice
Salt and freshly ground black pepper
½ cup pine nuts, chopped (optional)

Delicately toss all ingredients until well combined. Make sure not to bruise the lettuce. Season with salt and pepper to taste.

SERVES 4–6

Watercress and Broccoli, Green Goddess

If you have the patience and time, it is worth the effort to break the broccoli into tiny florets by hand, which results in a cleaner texture and flavor. This delicious dressing may also be used on other salads or dishes made up of heartier ingredients that can withhold its weight.

GREEN GODDESS DRESSING

1 avocado

3 tablespoons olive oil

1 tablespoon lemon juice

½ tablespoon cider vinegar

1 tablespoon agave

1 tablespoon minced fresh chives

1 teaspoon minced fresh tarragon

1 tablespoon chopped dulse or
  dulse flakes

½ teaspoon salt

¼ teaspoon pepper

1 cup water

SALAD

1 head broccoli, broken or chopped
  into small florets

3 cups fresh watercress

½ cup sunflower seeds

Salt and pepper

DRESSING Blend all ingredients in a high-speed blender until smooth and creamy.

FINISH Toss salad ingredients with enough dressing to generously coat. Season with salt and pepper to taste.

SERVES 4–6

Purslane, Sweet Pepper, Smoked Paprika

Purslane is a weed and happens to be the only plant source of B-12. We therefore recommend you enjoy it whenever possible.

RED PEPPER DRESSING

1 cup diced red pepper

1 tablespoon smoked paprika

2 tablespoons agave

2 tablespoons lemon juice

¼ cup olive oil

¼ cup water

Salt and pepper

4 to 5 cups purslane

Blend all ingredients for dressing in a high-speed blender until smooth. Toss with purslane and serve.

SERVES 4–6

Mexican Layer Salad

Everyone loves this colorful, vibrant layered salad. It's also on the menu at 105degrees at times.

CORN LAYER
3 cups fresh corn, cut from cob
1 red bell pepper, chopped
½ cup cilantro
1 tablespoon lemon juice
1 tablespoon lime juice
1 tablespoon olive oil
2 teaspoons cumin
Salt and pepper

AVOCADO/GUACAMOLE
2 large avocados
½ cup chopped fresh cilantro
2 tablespoons fresh lemon juice, or
   to taste
½ teaspoon kosher salt, or to taste
Pinch cayenne

PICO DE GALLO
1½ cups diced and seeded tomatoes
 2 tablespoons finely diced green
   onion
1 tablespoon diced jalapeños
2 tablespoons chopped cilantro
2 tablespoons lime juice
Salt and pepper

CORN LAYER Toss corn, bell pepper, and cilantro with remaining ingredients. Season with salt and pepper. Allow to marinate in refrigerator a few minutes before assembling.

AVOCADO/GUACAMOLE Mash together all ingredients in a bowl with a fork until semi-smooth, but fluffy. Season with coarse salt and a pinch of cayenne to taste.

PICO DE GALLO Toss all ingredients in a bowl. Salt and pepper to taste. Allow to marinate before assembling.

continued on page 68

Mexican Layer Salad
Continued

SOUR CREAM

2 cups cashews

1 cup water

¼ cup lemon juice

1 tablespoon nutritional yeast

1 teaspoon salt

CILANTRO LIME DRESSING

1 cup cilantro

½ cup extra virgin olive oil

½ cup lime juice

1 tablespoon apple cider vinegar

2 tablespoons honey

1 teaspoon salt

Pinch pepper

SALAD

6 cups romaine lettuce, coarsely
   chopped

SOUR CREAM Blend all ingredients in a high-speed blender until completely smooth.

CILANTRO LIME DRESSING Blend all ingredients in a high-speed blender until smooth and emulsified.

FINISH Preferably in a large glass serving dish or bowl, layer the ingredients in order listed or to your preference.

SERVES 4–6

Seaweed Salad

Seaweed salads benefit from slightly heavier and creamy dressings. Tahini and miso are great ingredients for any dressing that needs to have a bit more weight for coating more durable elements such as sea or root vegetables.

½ ounce wakame seaweed, cut or broken into small pieces
¼ ounce hijiki
3 tablespoons tahini
2 tablespoons lemon juice
1 tablespoon sesame oil
1 tablespoon miso
1 teaspoon grated ginger
¾ cup water
Sesame seeds or gomashio for garnish

SEAWEED Soak seaweed in warm water for at least 5 minutes. Drain, and strain out excess water.

DRESSING Blend tahini, lemon juice, sesame oil, miso, ginger, and water until smooth.

FINISH Toss seaweed with dressing. The salad is best if you allow it to marinate for at least 30 minutes. Garnish with sesame seeds or gomashio to serve.

SERVES 4–6

Thai Slaw, Kohlrabi, Basil, and Mint

If you are unable to find kohlrabi, this salad would also work well with any root vegetable, or a combination such as beet, carrot, and jicama.

THAI DRESSING

¼ cup cashews, soaked
⅓ cup sesame oil
¼ cup nama shoyu
¼ cup olive oil
¼ cup lime juice
2 tablespoons maple syrup, honey, or agave
2 tablespoons water (as needed)
2 teaspoons red chili flakes
Pinch salt
Pepper

SALAD

4 cups shredded kohlrabi, approximately 4 medium heads
¼ cup cilantro, chopped
¼ cup mint, chopped
¼ cup chopped cashews (for garnish)
Salt and pepper to taste

THAI DRESSING Blend all ingredients in a high-speed blender until smooth. Salt and pepper to taste.

FINISH Toss all salad ingredients together. Coat liberally with dressing. Season with salt and pepper to taste. For serving, garnish with a few pieces of mint and chopped cashews.

SERVES 4–6

Cucumber, Radish, and Avocado Chopped Salad

Subtle changes in how a vegetable is cut can make a dramatic difference in flavor and experience. The chunky texture of this salad holds up longer than other, more delicate options.

2 cups diced cucumber
(approximately ½-inch dice)
1 cup diced radish
2 diced avocados
¼ cup mint leaves, minced, or
microgreens
2 tablespoons lemon juice
1 tablespoon apple cider vinegar
2 tablespoons olive oil
Salt and pepper to taste

Toss all ingredients—the avocado should still be chunky, but provide a slight creaminess to the salad. Allow to marinate for approximately 10 minutes in the refrigerator before serving. Salt and pepper to taste.

SERVES 4–6

EXPRESS

& ROLLS

Nori, Jicama, Guacamole, Cucumber, Pineapple, Micro Herbs

Nori sheets are one of the best and most practical ingredients for making a quick wrap, and virtually all raw foods will taste great inside.

WRAPPER
1 medium jicama
12 sheets nori

GUACAMOLE
2 large avocados
2 tablespoons fresh lemon juice, or to taste
½ teaspoon kosher salt, or to taste
1 teaspoon wasabi powder (optional)

FILLING
½ fresh pineapple, peeled and julienned
1 cucumber, peeled and julienned
2 handfuls micro herbs (cilantro or basil)

Nama shoyu for serving (optional)

WRAPPER On a mandoline, slice jicama into paper-thin slices. Keep the slices as large and long as possible.

GUACAMOLE Mash together all ingredients in a bowl with a fork until semi-smooth, but fluffy. Use a bit of water if necessary, but keep the guacamole very thick. Season with coarse salt and wasabi to taste.

FINISH Line a bamboo rolling mat with saran wrap so that it stays clean and nothing will stick. Place a sheet of nori on the bamboo mat, shiny side against the mat. Lay out sheets of jicama on top of nori. Completely line the nori, making sure that each piece slightly overlaps so that when you roll, the wrap will not fall apart.

Place about ½ cup of guacamole on the jicama/nori and spread it out evenly across the bottom third of the sheet. Lay some of the pineapple, cucumber, and herbs across the guacamole. Leave some of the ingredients extending beyond the edges.

Gently fold the bottom of the bamboo mat up and over the filling and roll the nori tightly. You can use a little water to help seal the nori shut. Carefully unwrap the mat, and, using a very sharp knife, cut the roll into 6 to 8 pieces. Serve immediately with a little nama shoyu for dipping, if desired.

MAKES 12 SERVINGS

Collard, Citrus Miso Slaw, Avocado, Sunflower Sprouts

The best wraps have multiple personalities such as these collards—crunchy, creamy, rich, fresh, and flavorful.

DRESSING

½ cup cashews
⅓ cup tahini
¼ cup white miso
¼ cup orange juice
1 tablespoon lemon juice
1 tablespoon agave
1 tablespoon nama shoyu
3 to 4 tablespoons water (as needed to thin)
Salt and pepper

SLAW

½ head savoy cabbage, shredded

WRAPS

6 large collard leaves
1 avocado, thinly sliced
1 large carrot, julienned
Approximately 1 cup sunflower sprouts (or any type of sprout)
Salt and pepper to taste

SLAW AND DRESSING Blend all dressing ingredients in a high-speed blender until smooth. Generously coat cabbage with dressing. Save any excess dressing for dipping.

FINISH Cut out the center rib of each collard green leaf, dividing the leaf in half. Lay the leaf out flat with the underside facing up. Fill each leaf with a few tablespoons of the slaw mixture, avocado slices, carrot sticks, and sprouts. Season with salt and pepper. Serve with an extra drizzle of dressing on top or on the side.

MAKES 12 WRAPS

Spinach Zucchini Pizza Roll

This is a great finger food and a nice snack, especially for kids. Perfect for when you have leftover lasagna ingredients.

12 or more large spinach leaves, or other dark green leaves, stems removed

1 to 2 medium zucchinis, peeled and julienned

1 cup marinara (page 126)

1 cup Cilantro Walnut Pesto (page 94) or favorite pesto recipe

1 cup ricotta (page 116)

On each spinach leaf, layer a few pieces of zucchini, then add a few dollops of marinara, pesto, and ricotta.

MAKES 12 SERVINGS

Avocado Roll, Radish, Wasabi

The radishes and cucumber give this a nice, crisp bite.

12 sheets nori

Approximately 1 cup fresh radishes, peeled

2 cups guacamole (page 121)

1 cucumber, peeled and julienned

2 handfuls micro herbs (cilantro or basil)

Nama shoyu for serving (optional)

On a mandoline, thinly slice the radishes. Line a bamboo rolling mat with saran wrap so that it stays clean, and nothing will stick. Place a sheet of nori on the bamboo mat, shiny side against the mat. Lay out sheets of radishes on top of nori. Completely line the nori; make sure that each piece slightly overlaps so that when you roll, the wrap will not fall apart. (It is important to line the nori with the radishes so that it doesn't become soggy.)

Place about ½ cup of guacamole on the radishes/nori and spread out evenly across the bottom third of the sheet. Lay some of the cucumber and micro herbs across the guacamole. Leave some of the ingredients extending beyond the edges for a nice presentation.

Gently fold the bottom of the bamboo mat up and over the filling and roll the nori tightly. You can use a little water to help seal the nori shut. Carefully unwrap the mat, and using a very sharp knife, cut the roll into 6 to 8 pieces.

Serve immediately with a little nama shoyu for dipping, if desired.

MAKES 6–8 SERVINGS

Spicy Hand Roll, Daikon, Napa Cabbage, Carrots, Sprouts

Try other options for fillings including julienned beets, green papaya, green mango, and jicama.

DRESSING

1 cup almond butter

2 tablespoons nama shoyu

2 tablespoons grated ginger

1 tablespoon seeded and minced red chili

½ cup lemon juice

¼ cup agave

2 to 3 tablespoons water

SLAW

½ head napa cabbage, shredded

ROLL

6 sheets of nori, cut in half

1 daikon radish, peeled

1 carrot, julienned

1 red pepper, julienned

1 avocado, thinly sliced (optional)

Approximately 1 cup sprouts

SLAW AND DRESSING Blend all ingredients until smooth. Toss with cabbage.

FINISH On a mandoline, slice daikon into paper-thin slices. Keep the slices as large and long as possible. Lay out half sheets of nori with the shiny side facing down. Coat nori layer with thin slices of daikon. (It is important to line the nori with the daikon so that it doesn't become soggy.)

On one end of nori place a generous amount of slaw mixture. Layer in a few slices of carrot, red pepper, avocado (if using), and sprouts. Ideally you will be able to see the julienned vegetables when you roll it up. Gently roll nori at a diagonal to create a cone shape. If the nori won't stick to the other side you can use a little bit of water or nama shoyu to dampen it.

MAKES 12

Cucumber Roll, Goat Cheese, Mint Jam

These hold up surprisingly well, making them great for entertaining.

CUCUMBERS
2 to 3 medium to large cucumbers

GOAT CHEESE
1 cup cashews
1 cup macadamia nuts
1 tablespoon nutritional yeast
3 tablespoons lemon juice
1 teaspoon salt
1 teaspoon probiotic powder (optional)
Chives for garnish

MINT JAM
1 cup mint leaves
1 cup agave
2 tablespoons lemon juice
Pinch salt

WRAP Peel the cucumbers in alternating strips (you don't want the entire peel removed). Using a mandoline, cut the cucumber lengthwise into very thin slices.

GOAT CHEESE Blend all ingredients except chives in a high-speed blender until smooth. If using the probiotic powder, line a bowl with cheesecloth and allow mixture to drain at room temperature for 8 to 12 hours. Using the probiotic will make the cheese extra tart, but it is not a necessary step. If you aren't using the probiotic, you can serve the cheese immediately after blending.

MINT JAM Blend all ingredients in a high-speed blender until smooth.

FINISH Line a bamboo rolling mat with saran wrap so that it stays clean, and nothing will stick. Line the mat with long cucumber strips, slightly overlapping the strips so that the roll won't fall apart.

Place about ½ cup of goat cheese across the bottom half of mat (horizontally to the cucumber strips). Roll gently, forming a log. Keep the roll in saran wrap and place in the refrigerator for a few minutes in order to set before slicing.

When ready to serve, slice the roll into ½-inch-thick medallions and plate. Garnish with a few chives. Serve with mint jam on the side for dipping.

MAKES 12

Romaine, Sweet Pea Puree

As with so many raw recipes, the quality of the main ingredient is critical. For that reason, we recommend using high quality, fresh peas in season for this recipe. If they are not available, use frozen peas.

SWEET PEA PUREE

7 cups fresh or frozen peas, divided
1 avocado
1 tablespoon olive oil
1 tablespoon nutritional yeast
1 tablespoon agave
1 tablespoon lime juice
¼ cup chopped parsley
1 teaspoon nutmeg
1 teaspoon sea salt

WRAP

6 large romaine leaves
1 carrot, shaved into thin ribbons
  using a vegetable peeler
Chopped parsley for garnish
  (optional)

PEA PUREE Blend all ingredients except for 1 cup of peas in a high-speed blender until smooth. Stir in remaining peas. Salt and pepper to taste.

FINISH Spoon approximately ¼ cup pea puree into each romaine leaf. Garnish with shaved carrot and chopped parsley if desired.

MAKES 6 SERVINGS

Hummus Wrap

These are easy to make, great to have on hand, and super delicious for a fast lunch.

HUMMUS
4 cups peeled and chopped zucchini
1 cup tahini
1 cup lemon juice
6 tablespoons olive oil
3 to 4 tablespoons water
Salt and pepper

WRAP
6 to 12 large lettuce leaves (Swiss chard or romaine)
1 cup pitted, chopped sun-dried olives
4 tablespoons chopped fresh herbs (parsley, basil, mint)
Salt and pepper
Olive oil for garnish

HUMMUS Blend all ingredients in a high-speed blender until smooth. Season with salt and pepper to taste.

FINISH Fill each lettuce leaf with a generous amount of hummus. Top with a few chopped olives and garnish with fresh herbs. To finish, season with salt, pepper, and an extra drizzle of olive oil.

MAKES 6–12 WRAPS

Swiss Chard Reuben Roll, Sauerkraut, Thousand Island Dressing

We love tempeh reubens and this raw version with mushrooms is a great replacement for that craving. This recipe is also delicious with avocado.

MUSHROOMS

2 portobello mushroom caps, stems removed, sliced into ¼-inch-thick strips

1 tablespoon olive oil

1 tablespoon nama shoyu

1 tablespoon lemon juice

Salt

THOUSAND ISLAND DRESSING

1 cup cashews

2 tomatoes, chopped

2 red bell peppers, seeded and chopped

1 cup chopped celery

2 tablespoons olive oil

1 tablespoon miso

¼ cup lemon juice

2 tablespoons apple cider vinegar

1 tablespoon agave

Approximately 1 cup water

Salt and pepper

WRAP

6 large Swiss chard leaves, stems removed, sliced in half

1 cup or more fresh sauerkraut

MUSHROOMS Toss mushrooms with olive oil, nama shoyu, lemon juice, and salt. Allow to marinate at least 30 minutes before serving.

DRESSING Blend all ingredients in a high-speed blender until smooth. Add more or less water depending on how thick you like your dressing. Season with salt and pepper to taste.

FINISH Using a Swiss chard leaf as a wrap, fill with a generous portion of sauerkraut and a few marinated mushroom slices. Drizzle with dressing before wrapping, or use dressing as a side dip.

MAKES 12 WRAPS

EXPRESS

Carrot Ribbons, Sweet Tomatoes

Summery, refreshing, and light, this dish also works well when you substitute various colors of carrot, golden beets, or other root vegetables.

SWEET TOMATO SAUCE

¼ cup olive oil

3 cups chopped tomatoes
(heirlooms if possible)

¼ cup agave

2 tablespoons lemon juice

2 teaspoons salt

Pepper to taste

¼ cup basil, julienned

NOODLES

1 cup cherry tomatoes, halved

8 cups chopped carrots, run
through a spiral slicer

GARNISH

12 basil leaves, julienned

¼ cup pine nuts

SWEET TOMATO SAUCE Blend all ingredients except basil in a high-speed blender until smooth. Stir in basil. Season with salt and pepper.

ASSEMBLY Toss tomato sauce with cherry tomato halves and carrot ribbons. Garnish with basil and pine nuts.

SERVES 4–6

"Pho," Spring Vegetables, Bean Sprouts

Kelp noodles, available online and in some gourmet shops, are incredibly versatile and helpful in recipes that include a flavored broth or sauce.

BROTH

½ cup nama shoyu

½ cup sesame oil

¼ cup fresh lime juice

¼ cup fresh orange juice

½ cup agave

1 tablespoon grated ginger

1 tablespoon grated lemongrass (optional)

1 tablespoon miso

1 teaspoon cinnamon

1 teaspoon star anise

½ cup kelp noodles

Pinch salt and pepper

VEGETABLES

½ cup zucchini noodles (long, thin juliennes, preferably cut on a mandoline)

½ cup carrot noodles (long, thin juliennes, preferably cut on a mandoline)

½ cup broccoli florets

¼ cup thinly sliced red bell pepper

¼ cup mung bean sprouts

1 tablespoon sesame oil

1 tablespoon sesame seeds

1 tablespoon lemon juice

Cilantro for garnish

BROTH Blend all ingredients for broth except kelp in a high-speed blender until smooth. Add about half of the kelp and blend until smooth; add more or less depending on your preference. Kelp has a very distinct flavor. Season with salt and pepper to taste.

ASSEMBLY Toss vegetables with sesame oil, sesame seeds, and lemon juice. Divide vegetables evenly among 4 to 6 bowls, reserving some for garnish. Top with broth and garnish with remaining vegetables and cilantro.

SERVES 4–6

Parsnip Noodles, Cilantro Walnut Pesto

Wintery and satisfying, there are many variations of this recipe, substituting various herbs, nuts, and root vegetables. Experiment!

NOODLES
4 to 5 large parsnips
Salt

CILANTRO WALNUT PESTO
2 cups cilantro, stems removed
1/2 cup walnuts, plus more for garnish
3 tablespoons lemon juice
1 tablespoon nutritional yeast
1/2 teaspoon seeded and chopped serrano chile
1/2 teaspoon coarse salt
Pepper
1/4 cup olive oil

NOODLES Run parsnips through a spiral slicer to yield approximately 8 cups. Toss parsnip noodles with a few teaspoons of salt and allow to wilt for at least 10 minutes. Rinse, drain, and dry noodles well.

PESTO Pulse all ingredients in a food processor and blend until well combined but still slightly chunky.

FINISH Toss noodles with pesto. Season with salt and pepper. Garnish with a few chopped walnuts before serving.

SERVES 4–6

Zucchini, Lemon, Tahini

NOODLES

Approximately 4 large zucchini

TAHINI SAUCE

½ cup tahini

¼ cup lemon juice

2 tablespoons olive oil

1½ cups water

¼ teaspoon salt

Pepper

GARNISH

1 cup pitted and chopped sun-dried olives

3 tablespoons chopped fresh herbs (basil, mint, cilantro, parsley)

NOODLES Peel zucchini and run through a spiral slicer. This should yield about 8 cups.

TAHINI SAUCE Blend all ingredients in a high-speed blender until smooth. Season with salt and pepper to taste.

ASSEMBLY Toss noodles, sauce, olives, and herbs until well combined.

SERVES 4–6

Butternut Squash Alfredo, Wilted Spinach, Wild Mushrooms, Savory

Savory is an excellent and delicate herb; paired with the squash it makes a luxurious dish.

NOODLES
1 large butternut squash
Salt

WILTED SPINACH
5 to 6 cups baby spinach
2 tablespoons olive oil
2 tablespoons lemon juice
Salt and pepper

ALFREDO
2 cups cashews or 1½ cups
   cashews and ½ cup pine nuts
2 tablespoons lemon juice
1 tablespoon white miso
1 tablespoon agave
1½ cups water
1 tablespoon thyme
¼ teaspoon salt
¼ teaspoon pepper

MUSHROOMS
2 cups stemmed and chopped
   mushrooms (cremini, shiitake,
   oyster, portobello)
2 tablespoons olive oil
2 tablespoons nama shoyu
1 tablespoon minced fresh savory

NOODLES Run the squash through a spiral slicer on medium spiral. Toss squash noodles with a few teaspoons of salt and allow to wilt for at least 10 minutes. Rinse, drain, and dry noodles well before tossing them with sauce.

SPINACH With clean hands, toss the spinach with the remaining ingredients. Gently massage to "wilt" the spinach. Season with salt and pepper to taste.

ALFREDO Blend all ingredients in a high-speed blender until smooth.

MUSHROOMS Toss mushrooms with olive oil and nama shoyu. Allow to marinate approximately 30 minutes before serving.

ASSEMBLY Toss drained noodles with spinach and mushrooms, then gradually add a generous amount of Alfredo sauce. Toss in fresh savory. Season with salt and pepper to taste.

SERVES 4–6

Yellow Squash, "Pad Thai," Chives, Cashews

NOODLES

4 yellow squash

SAUCE

2 tablespoons tahini

2 tablespoons almond butter

2 tablespoons nama shoyu

½ cup lemon juice

2 tablespoons olive oil

1 tablespoon agave, maple syrup, or honey

1 cup water

Minced fresh red chile (optional)

GARNISH

2 tablespoons chopped chives

2 tablespoons chopped cashews

NOODLES Run squash through a spiral slicer. This will yield approximately 8 cups.

SAUCE Blend all ingredients for sauce in a high-speed blender until smooth.

ASSEMBLY Just before serving, toss sauce with squash noodles. Garnish with chopped chives and cashews.

SERVES 4–6

Spicy Sesame Noodles

Feel free to adjust the heat if you prefer, by using additional red chile.

SAUCE

1 cup cashews
1 cup water (or more if you prefer a
   thinner sauce)
2 tablespoons tahini
¼ cup lemon juice
2 tablespoons nama shoyu
2 tablespoons grated ginger
2 tablespoons seeded and minced
   red chile
¼ cup agave

NOODLES

Approximately 8 cups kelp noodles,
   rinsed and drained well

GARNISH

¼ cup chopped cashews
1 bunch chives, finely chopped

SAUCE Blend all ingredients in a high-speed blender until smooth and creamy.

ASSEMBLY Toss sauce with kelp noodles. Garnish with cashews and chives to serve.

SERVES 4–6

Zucchini, Sweet Corn Pesto, Mint

For a more rustic (and in our opinion, more flavorful) option, try making this the old-fashioned way, with mortar and pestle.

NOODLES
4 large zucchini

SWEET CORN PESTO
5 cups corn kernels, divided
¼ cup pine nuts
½ cup mint, chopped
1 teaspoon salt
Pepper to taste
½ cup olive oil

NOODLES Peel and run zucchini through a spiral slicer. This should yield about 8 cups.

SWEET CORN PESTO Process all ingredients except olive oil and 1 cup corn in a food processor until well combined and chunky. With machine running, add olive oil. Stir in remaining cup of corn. Taste and season with salt and pepper.

ASSEMBLY Toss pesto with zucchini noodles and serve immediately.

SERVES 4–6

Kelp Udon, Mushroom Broth, Cabbage, Shiitakes

MUSHROOM BROTH

3 cups warm water

4 ounces dried shiitake

1 cup cremini (or button) mushrooms

½ cup nama shoyu

2 tablespoons brown rice vinegar

2 tablespoons lemon juice

1 tablespoon sesame oil

1 tablespoon agave

NOODLES

2 packages kelp noodles

½ head napa cabbage, thinly sliced

2 tablespoons sesame seeds

2 tablespoons finely sliced scallions

BROTH Pour water over dried shiitakes. Allow mushrooms to soften for approximately 30 minutes. Keep the mushroom soaking liquid. Once mushrooms are soft, remove stems and then chop. Blend mushroom soaking liquid, chopped shiitakes, fresh mushrooms, and remaining ingredients in a high-speed blender until smooth.

ASSEMBLY Drain and rinse kelp noodles. Stir noodles and cabbage into mushroom broth. Garnish each serving with sesame seeds and scallions.

SERVES 4–6

Spaghetti and Meatballs

NOODLES

4 large zucchini

MARINARA

1½ cups sun-dried tomatoes,
   soaked approximately 30 minutes
   (1 hour is better)
1 roma tomato, chopped
1 tablespoon lemon juice
1 tablespoon chopped fresh basil
2 tablespoons olive oil
1 tablespoon agave
Pinch salt
Pinch red pepper flakes

MEATBALLS

2 cups stemmed and chopped
   cremini mushrooms
1 tablespoons olive oil
½ tablespoon nama shoyu
¼ cup tahini
¼ cup walnuts
2 tablespoons chopped parsley
Salt and pepper to taste

GARNISH

3 to 4 tablespoons freshly
   minced basil

NOODLES Peel zucchini and run it through a spiral slicer. This should yield about 8 cups.

MARINARA Drain water from sun-dried tomatoes and place all ingredients in a high-speed blender. Process until smooth.

MEATBALLS In a high-speed blender, process ingredients until well combined but still chunky. Using a rounded tablespoon, form into small "meatballs."

ASSEMBLY Toss zucchini noodles with marinara. Season with salt and pepper to taste. Serve each dish with a few meatballs. Garnish with basil before serving.

SERVES 4–6

EXPRESS

ÉES

Squash Blossom Tamales, Sweet Pea Puree, Sour Cream, Pico

Our earlier tamale recipes all use corn husks and a raw masa. While we love that method, this is faster and lighter—and great for warm weather.

SWEET PEA PUREE

6 cups fresh peas
1 avocado
1 tablespoon olive oil
1 tablespoon nutritional yeast
1 tablespoon agave
1 tablespoon lime juice
¼ cup chopped cilantro
1 teaspoon nutmeg
¼ teaspoon cayenne*
1 teaspoon sea salt

BLOSSOMS

At least 1 dozen squash blossoms,
   rinsed, with stems removed

GARNISH

Queso Fresco (page 122)
Pico de Gallo (page 121)
Guacamole (page 121)

*A little bit of cayenne goes a
long way.

In a food processor, process all ingredients for Sweet Pea Puree until well combined and slightly chunky. Fill squash blossoms with a few table-spoons of puree. Before serving, drizzle with Sour Cream. Serve with Pico de Gallo and Guacamole as condiments.

MAKES 12

Spring Vegetable Couscous, Fava

While we include a number of ingredients in the vegetable portion of this recipe, do not hesitate to use more of something you like or remove an ingredient that is not readily available.

COUSCOUS
2 large heads cauliflower
2/3 cup pine nuts
2 tablespoons nutritional yeast
2 tablespoons olive oil
1 tablespoon agave
Salt and pepper

VEGETABLES
1 cup fava beans, peeled
1 cup corn (preferably fresh)
1 cup finely diced carrots
1 cup diced cremini mushrooms
1 cup diced zucchini
1/4 cup minced parsley
2 tablespoons minced basil
2 tablespoons olive oil
1 tablespoon lemon juice
Salt and pepper

SAUCE
1/2 cup nama shoyu
1/4 cup lemon juice
1 tablespoon apple cider vinegar
3 tablespoons agave
1 tablespoon olive oil

COUSCOUS Pulse all ingredients in a high-speed blender until cauliflower florets are very fine and all ingredients are well combined.

VEGETABLES Toss all ingredients until well combined.

SAUCE Blend all ingredients in a high-speed blender until smooth and well emulsified.

FINISH Toss couscous with vegetable medley. Spoon a few heaping tablespoons of sauce over the mixture before serving. If plating individually, drizzle each serving with more sauce or serve as a side.

SERVES 4–6

Portobello Steak, Wilted Spinach

Raw food for an omnivore.

MUSHROOMS
4 to 6 portobello mushroom caps
3 tablespoons olive oil
2 tablespoons balsamic vinegar
Salt and pepper

SPINACH
5 to 6 cups baby spinach
2 tablespoons olive oil
2 tablespoons lemon juice
Salt and pepper

MUSHROOMS Gently toss mushrooms with remaining ingredients and allow to marinate for at least 30 minutes before serving.

SPINACH With clean hands, toss the spinach with the remaining ingredients. Gently massage to "wilt" the spinach. Season with salt and pepper to taste.

FINISH Serve components separately on the plate, or "stack" by placing spinach mixture on top of mushrooms. Drizzle with a little extra olive oil and season with salt and pepper before serving.

SERVES 4–6

Vegetable Napoleon

The idea of layering is not simply about presentation or complexity. When food is stacked, the palate experiences multiple flavors and textures in a compelling way.

MUSHROOMS

4 to 6 portobello mushroom caps

3 tablespoons olive oil

2 tablespoons balsamic vinegar

Salt and pepper

VEGETABLES

1 to 2 large heirloom tomatoes
  (enough for 4 to 6 large slices)

1 large avocado, thinly sliced

Lemon juice

Olive oil

Salt and pepper

2 tablespoons chopped basil

MUSHROOMS Gently toss mushrooms with remaining ingredients and allow to marinate for at least 30 minutes before serving.

FINISH Plate one mushroom per plate, with underside facing up. Layer with a large slice of tomato and a few slices of avocado. Sprinkle serving with fresh basil, and drizzle with a little lemon juice and olive oil. Season generously with freshly ground salt and pepper. Garnish with chopped basil.

SERVES 4–6

Green Tomato Pave, Pistachio Relish, Sweet Tomato Fondue

Green tomatoes, when available, are a bit more firm and hold up well to presentations involving layering—we love the way they look and taste.

TOMATOES
8 large green tomatoes*

SWEET TOMATO FONDUE
¼ cup olive oil
3 cups chopped tomatoes (heirlooms if possible)
¼ cup agave
2 tablespoons lemon juice
2 teaspoons salt
Pepper to taste
¼ cup basil, julienned, plus more for garnish

PISTACHIO RELISH
1 cup pistachios
¼ cup lemon juice
¼ cup olive oil
1 teaspoon salt
Pepper

*Red or yellow tomatoes can be substituted, although they are not as firm.

TOMATOES Thinly slice tomatoes on a mandoline.

SWEET TOMATO FONDUE Blend all ingredients except basil in a high-speed blender until smooth. Stir in basil.

RELISH Pulse all ingredients in a high-speed blender until well combined but still chunky. Season with salt and pepper to taste.

FINISH Alternate layering 3 to 4 tomatoes with Pistachio Relish. Drizzle with Sweet Tomato Fondue. Garnish with more Pistachio Relish and a few pieces of fresh basil. Serve immediately.

SERVES 4–6

Trumpet Scallops, Barbeque Miso Glaze

King trumpet mushrooms have great flavor and texture and are one of the best mushrooms to use for raw food.

MUSHROOMS
Approximately 1 dozen large king
   trumpet mushrooms

GLAZE
½ cup miso paste
½ cup nama shoyu
½ cup agave
2 tablespoons apple cider vinegar
2 tablespoons lemon juice
2 tablespoons water
2 teaspoons sesame oil

MUSHROOMS Slice off both ends of mushrooms. You want a fairly even white stalk to work with. Slice mushrooms crosswise into medallions that are approximately ½ inch thick. These make the scallops. You should get at least 4 slices per mushroom depending on how large the mushrooms are.

GLAZE Blend all ingredients in a high-speed blender until smooth.

FINISH Toss mushroom scallops with glaze and allow to marinate at least 30 minutes before serving. Serve 4 to 6 scallops per person. Drizzle with extra glaze if desired.

SERVES 4–6

Poblanos, Corn Pudding, Sweet Pepper Crema

Although optional, we highly recommend any or all of the following with this: Guacamole, Sour Cream, and Pico de Gallo.

POBLANOS
2 to 3 small to medium poblano peppers, cut in half, stems and seeds removed
1 tablespoon lemon juice
Olive oil
Salt

CORN PUDDING
2 cups fresh or frozen corn kernels
2 cups peeled and chopped zucchini
1 cup seeded and chopped red pepper
1 tablespoon cilantro
1 tablespoon minced jalapeño (or less)
2 tablespoons olive oil
1 tablespoon lime juice
¼ teaspoon cumin
¼ teaspoon chili powder
Pinch cayenne
Salt and pepper

POBLANOS Toss the peppers with lemon juice and a touch of olive oil and salt. Allow to marinate for 30 minutes to break down some of the fibers and soften. Rinse peppers under cool water and dry before serving.

CORN PUDDING Pulse all ingredients in a food processor until well combined but slightly chunky. Season with salt and pepper to taste.

FINISH Fill each pepper half with a generous amount of corn pudding. Garnish with an extra drizzle of olive oil or Cilantro Oil (page 124). Serve with a side of Guacamole (page 121), Sour Cream (page 122), and Pico de Gallo (page 121) if desired.

SERVES 4–6

Wild Mushroom Lasagna, Butternut Squash, Wilted Spinach

We've done a version of this at 105degrees that calls for dehydrating, but it works quite well without in this case.

SQUASH
1 large or 2 small butternut squash
Olive oil
Salt

RICOTTA
2 cups pine nuts or cashews
3 tablespoons lemon juice
2 tablespoons nutritional yeast
1 teaspoon sea salt
1 teaspoon black pepper

MUSHROOMS
1½ cups stemmed and chopped shiitake mushrooms
1½ cups stemmed and chopped cremini mushrooms
1 cup stemmed and chopped oyster mushrooms
3 tablespoons olive oil
1 tablespoon lemon juice
1 tablespoon nama shoyu
Salt and pepper

SPINACH
5 to 6 cups baby spinach
1 tablespoon minced oregano, plus more for garnish
1 tablespoon thyme, plus more for garnish
2 tablespoons olive oil
2 tablespoons lemon juice
Salt and pepper

SQUASH Peel squash, cut into quarters, and remove seeds. Using a mandoline or vegetable peeler, cut the squash lengthwise into very thin slices. You want each slice to be approximately 3 inches long. Toss with a generous amount of olive oil and salt. Allow to soften for at least 30 minutes. Rinse and drain before using.

RICOTTA Pulse all ingredients in a high-speed blender until smooth and fluffy.

MUSHROOMS Toss mushrooms with remaining ingredients and allow to marinate for 30 minutes or less.

SPINACH With clean hands, toss the spinach with remaining ingredients. Gently massage to "wilt" the spinach. Season with salt and pepper to taste.

FINISH Place 2 to 3 slices of butternut squash, slightly overlapping, in the center of each plate. Spread on a generous amount of ricotta. Layer with wilted spinach, then mushroom medley. Repeat once more. Garnish with oregano and thyme. Drizzle with a little olive oil, salt, and freshly ground pepper before serving.

SERVES 4–6

EXPRESS
CONDI

MENTS

Golden Raisin Relish

This relish goes well with many of our recipes, such as curried soup or other dishes that are both spicy and sweet.

¾ cup plump golden raisins
1 tablespoon minced ginger
1½ teaspoons agave
¼ teaspoon mustard seeds
¼ teaspoon cayenne pepper
¼ teaspoon salt
¼ cup apple cider vinegar

Pulse all ingredients in a high-speed blender until well combined but still chunky. Store in the refrigerator.

MAKES ABOUT 1 CUP

Jalapeño Parsley Pesto

In the summer when vibrant peppers are available in a multitude of colors and various degrees of heat, there are unlimited options for this recipe.

1 bunch parsley
¼ cup pine nuts
1 tablespoon lime juice
1 tablespoon agave
½ jalapeño pepper, seeded
  and diced
3 tablespoons nutritional yeast
¼ cup olive oil
1 teaspoon salt
Pepper

Process all ingredients except olive oil in a high-speed blender until combined and chunky. With machine running, add olive oil. Season with salt and pepper to taste.

MAKES ABOUT 1 CUP

Guacamole

Guacamole can be made with a mortar and pestle, although we recommend using a fork, which adds to its fluffy texture.

2 large avocados
½ cup chopped fresh cilantro
2 tablespoons fresh lemon juice, or to taste
½ teaspoon kosher salt, or to taste
Pinch cayenne
Water if necessary

Mash all ingredients together in a bowl with a fork until semismooth, but fluffy. Use a bit of water if necessary. Season with coarse salt and a pinch of cayenne to taste.

MAKES 2–4 SERVINGS

Pico de Gallo

Pico is an all-purpose condiment that works equally well with different varieties of tomatoes and even serrano chiles.

1½ cups diced and seeded tomatoes
2 tablespoons finely diced green onion
1 tablespoon diced jalapeños
2 tablespoons chopped cilantro
2 tablespoons lime juice
Kosher salt
Pepper

Toss all ingredients in a bowl. Season with salt and pepper to taste. Allow to marinate before serving.

MAKES ABOUT 2 CUPS

Quick Cucumber Pickles

These are great to have on hand for snacks or on salads.

3 cups thinly sliced cucumbers
3 tablespoons salt
¼ cup agave
¼ cup apple cider vinegar
1 tablespoon celery seed
1 tablespoon mustard seed

Slice cucumbers on a mandoline; toss with remaining ingredients. Allow to marinate at least 30 minutes before serving.

MAKES ABOUT 3 CUPS

Sour Cream (Queso Fresco)

This can be made in 30 minutes. If you do decide to dehydrate it for a couple of hours, however, the result will be more like goat cheese.

2 cups cashews
1 cup water
¼ cup lemon juice
1 tablespoon nutritional yeast
1 teaspoon salt

Blend all ingredients in a high-speed blender until completely smooth.

MAKES ABOUT 2 CUPS

Quick Cucumber Pickles

Cilantro Oil

Herbal oils are a quick and easy finish for dishes that require extra, subtle flavor. They also add a burst of color to presentations.

2 cups cilantro, stems removed
1 cup olive oil
1 teaspoon sea salt

Blend all ingredients in a high-speed blender until mostly smooth. Strain out solids through a cheesecloth.

MAKES ABOUT 2 CUPS

Gomashio

You can purchase gomashio at the store, but preparing it yourself allows for the creation of your own balance of flavors and ensures freshness. It's great on nearly everything and a perfect way to reduce the need for salt.

½ cup sesame seeds
1 tablespoon sea salt
2 tablespoons kelp, hijiki, or any
  dried seaweed

Grind all ingredients in a spice grinder until mixture is well combined. Use for sprinkling and seasoning in place of salt.

MAKES ½ CUP

Cilantro Oil

Harissa

This North African condiment brings a smoky, rich element to dishes that benefit from spice and deep flavor contrast.

10 to 12 dried red chili peppers
½ teaspoon salt
2 tablespoons olive oil
1 teaspoon smoked paprika
1 teaspoon ground coriander
1 teaspoon ground caraway seeds
½ teaspoon cumin

Soak the dried chilis in warm water. Remove stems and seeds. Combine all ingredients in a high-speed blender until a fairly smooth paste forms. Store in an airtight container with a little extra olive oil to keep fresh.

MAKES ABOUT ½ CUP

EXPRESS

Blueberry Sherbet

This would also make a great smoothie with a bit more liquid. Looking at the recipe from that perspective may help in understanding the concept behind making frozen desserts.

2 cups blueberries, fresh or frozen, plus more for serving
1¼ cups nut milk
¾ cup cashews
½ cup agave, maple syrup, or honey
2 tablespoons vanilla
1 teaspoon hazelnut extract
½ cup coconut butter
Pinch salt

Blend all ingredients in a high-speed blender until smooth. Run through an ice cream maker according to manufacturer's directions. Layer with more blueberries to serve.

SERVES 4–6

Banana Chia Pudding

Chia seeds lend an expansive and gelatinous quality to recipes requiring a creamy texture, such as puddings. Their texture is also very pleasant.

½ cup chia seeds
1 cup cashews
1 cup water
1 cup mashed banana
½ cup honey
1 tablespoon cinnamon
¼ teaspoon nutmeg
¼ teaspoon ginger
1 teaspoon vanilla
1 vanilla bean, scraped
¼ teaspoon salt

Blend all ingredients except for the chia seeds in a high-speed blender until smooth, making a cashew crème. Pour crème over chia seeds and allow to soak for at least 30 minutes and up to 2 hours or more until the chia becomes a tapioca consistency.

Note: You can add fresh fruit or dried fruit and nuts to your liking for a delicious breakfast.

SERVES 4–6

Spiced Pineapple with Rose Water and Pistachios

Mango is a great alternative in this refreshing recipe.

1 pineapple, ends removed
  and peeled
½ cup agave
½ teaspoon cinnamon
2 tablespoons rose water
1 tablespoon lemon juice
¼ cup chopped pistachios
Pinch coarse salt

Thinly slice the pineapple into pieces ¼ to ⅙ inch thick. Mix agave, cinnamon, rose water, and lemon juice. Drizzle pineapple slices with liquid mixture. Allow to marinate in the refrigerator a few minutes before serving.

Serve 4 to 5 slices per person. Arrange on plates and garnish with chopped pistachios and coarse salt.

SERVES 4–6

Hemp Milk

1 cup hemp seeds
5 cups water
2 tablespoons agave

Blend all ingredients in a high-speed blender until smooth, at least 2 minutes. If desired, strain through a cheesecloth, but for all the good fiber of hemp leave as is.

MAKES 5 CUPS

Spiced Pineapple with
Rose Water and Pistachios

Chocolate Hemp Milk Custard (Nut Free)

Everyone is surprised and amazed by this rich dessert. It truly has the consistency of a traditional chocolate pudding or mousse and is both nut and coconut free. Best of all, it takes only moments to prepare.

2 avocados, mashed
1 cup Hemp Milk (page 134)
1 cup agave
1 cup cocoa powder
2 teaspoons vanilla
¼ teaspoon cinnamon
Pinch salt

Blend all ingredients in a high-speed blender until smooth. If preferred cool, chill in glasses or bowls before serving.

SERVES 4–6

Banana Gelato

An even simpler variation on this can be made with frozen bananas, simply by running them through a champion juicer.

3 cups banana chunks, frozen
1¼ cups water (or nut milk for a creamier consistency)
½ cup agave, maple syrup, or honey
2 tablespoons vanilla
1 tablespoon lemon juice
½ cup coconut butter
Pinch salt

Blend all ingredients in a high-speed blender until smooth. Run through an ice cream maker according to manufacturer's directions.

SERVES 4–6

Chocolate Hemp Milk
Custard (Nut Free)

Maple Crème Brûlée

While we recommend agave or honey for most dessert recipes, maple syrup has a silky richness that is ideal for more decadent desserts.

1½ cups cashews
½ cup pine nuts
½ cup maple syrup
⅔ cup coconut oil, melted
1 teaspoon lemon juice
¼ teaspoon salt
2 vanilla beans, scraped
1 teaspoon vanilla
Maple syrup for serving

Blend cashews, pine nuts, and ½ cup maple syrup in a high-speed blender until smooth. Add all other ingredients, aside from remaining maple syrup, and continue to blend until smooth. Do not overblend.

Pour mixture into a flan mold, or any smooth-sided ramekin, and allow to set in freezer for 30 minutes. Once dessert is set, refrigerate. When firm, turn over and remove from ramekin. After plated, drizzle each dish with approximately 2 tablespoons maple syrup.

SERVES 6

Lemon Bavarois, Raspberry Syrup

Bavarois is another term for Bavarian Crème. It is a thick, creamy custard that is usually made with heavy cream and gelatin.

BAVAROIS

2 cups cashews, soaked
½ cup lemon juice
⅔ cup agave
⅔ cup coconut oil, melted
½ teaspoon salt
¼ cup lemon zest
1 vanilla bean, scraped

RASPBERRY SYRUP

2 cups raspberries
6–8 tablespoons maple syrup or
   agave
2 tablespoons lemon zest

GARNISH

2 tablespoons orange zest

Blend cashews, lemon juice, and agave in a high-speed blender until smooth. Gradually add coconut oil and remaining ingredients; continue to blend until smooth. Fill serving dishes half full and allow to set in freezer until partially set.

Meanwhile, make Raspberry Syrup by blending all ingredients in a high-speed blender until smooth. Pour syrup over partially set Bavarois and top with more Bavarois. Return to freezer until set.

Remove from freezer and garnish with orange zest to serve.

SERVES 6–8

index

Metric Conversion Chart

VOLUME MEASUREMENTS		WEIGHT MEASUREMENTS		TEMPERATURE CONVERSION	
U.S.	METRIC	U.S.	METRIC	FAHRENHEIT	CELSIUS
1 teaspoon	5 ml	½ ounce	15 g	250	120
1 tablespoon	15 ml	1 ounce	30 g	300	150
¼ cup	60 ml	3 ounces	90 g	325	160
⅓ cup	75 ml	4 ounces	115 g	350	180
½ cup	125 ml	8 ounces	225 g	375	190
⅔ cup	150 ml	12 ounces	350 g	400	200
¾ cup	175 ml	1 pound	450 g	425	220
1 cup	250 ml	2¼ pounds	1 kg	450	230